Let's Explore the Seasons

by Laura Hamilton Waxman

BUMBA BOOKS™

LERNER PUBLICATIONS ◆ MINNEAPOLIS

Note to Educators

Throughout this book, you'll find critical-thinking questions. These can be used to engage young readers in thinking critically about the topic and in using the text and photos to do so.

For Bryn and Cassie, who bring joy season after season

Lerner Publications Company
An imprint of Lerner Publishing Group, Inc.
241 First Avenue North
Minneapolis, MN 55401 USA

For reading levels and more information, look up this title at www.lernerbooks.com.

Main body text set in Helvetica Textbook Com Roman.
Typeface provided by Linotype AG.

Library of Congress Cataloging-in-Publication Data

Names: Waxman, Laura Hamilton, author.
Title: Let's explore the seasons / Laura Hamilton Waxman.
Description: Minneapolis : Lerner Publications, [2022] | Series: Bumba books - Let's explore nature's cycles |
    Includes bibliographical references and index. | Audience: Ages 4–7 | Audience: Grades K–1 | Summary:
    "Emerging readers learn about the qualities of and vocabulary associated with the four seasons"— Provided by
    publisher.
Identifiers: LCCN 2020009441 (print) | LCCN 2020009442 (ebook) | ISBN 9781728404042 (library binding) |
    ISBN 9781728417745 (ebook)
Subjects: LCSH: Seasons—Juvenile literature.
Classification: LCC QB637.4 .W39 2021 (print) | LCC QB637.4 (ebook) | DDC 508.2—dc23

LC record available at https://lccn.loc.gov/2020009441
LC ebook record available at https://lccn.loc.gov/2020009442

Manufactured in the United States of America
1-48462-48976-11/2/2020

Table of Contents

Four Seasons

The year has four seasons.

Fall, winter, spring, and summer follow one after another.

The seasons repeat in a cycle year after year.

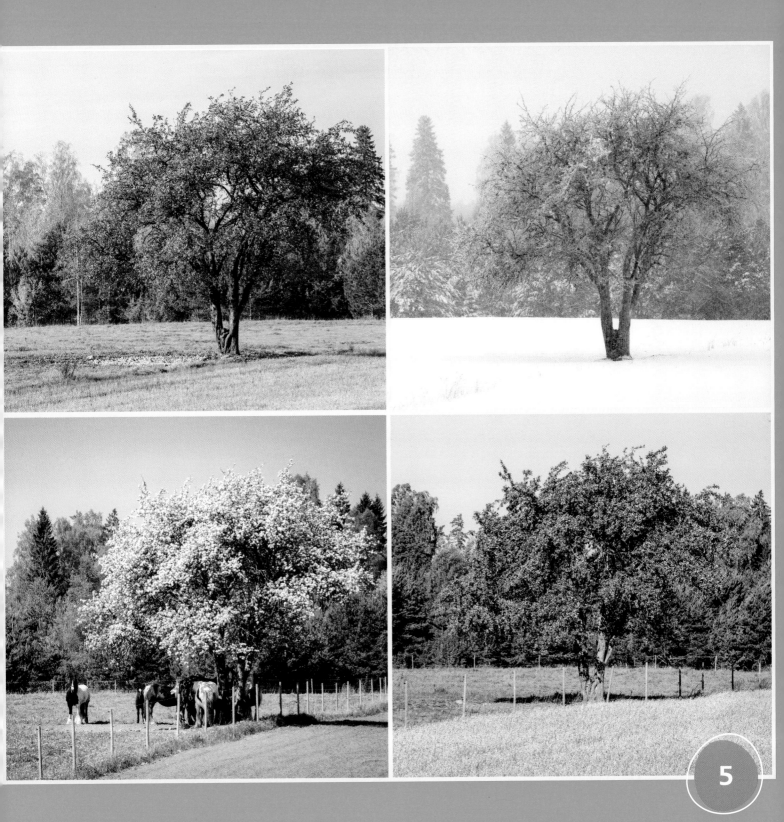

It's fall.

The air is cool.

Many trees are losing

their leaves.

Some animals gather food

for the winter.

Others migrate to warmer

parts of the world.

Winter has come.

The air is chilly.

Snow falls from the sky.

Some animals hibernate or stay underground. Others grow thick fur to keep warm.

How do you stay warm in winter?

It's spring.

The cold air and snow

are gone.

Here comes the rain.

The rain and warm air help plants grow.

Tree branches sprout new buds.

Migrating animals return for the warm weather.

Which animals can you see and hear in the spring?

Next comes summer.

It's hot outside.

A warm breeze blows flowers,

grass, and leaves.

After summer is fall.

The air begins to cool.

Leaves drop from trees.

The cycle of the seasons

continues.

The Cycle of Seasons

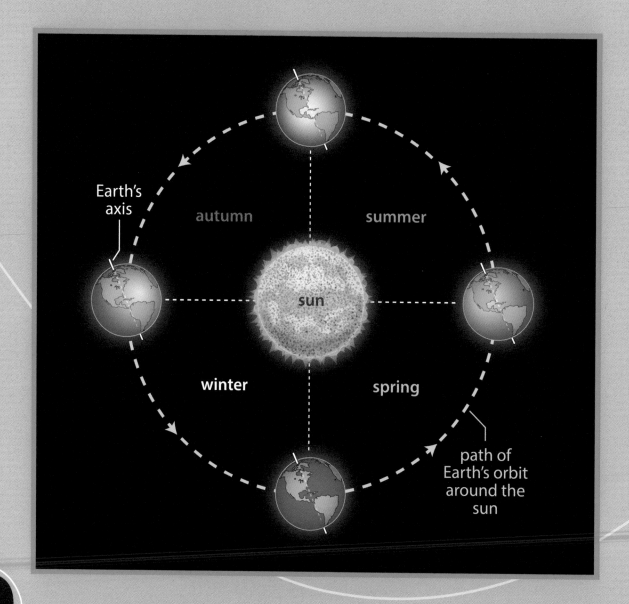

Picture Glossary

bud

a small, new leaf that grows into a bigger leaf

cycle

something that repeats again and again

hibernate

to sleep or rest for part or all of winter

migrate

to go from one part of the world to another when the seasons change

Learn More

Carlson-Berne, Emma. *Let's Explore Migration*. Minneapolis: Lerner Publications, 2022.

Lynch, Annabelle. *Seasons*. New York: Windmill Books, 2016.

Salas, Laura Purdie. *Snack, Snooze, Skedaddle: How Animals Get Ready for Winter*. Minneapolis: Milbrook Press, 2019.

Index

Photo Credits

Image credits: FotoHelin/Shutterstock.com, pp. 5, 23 (top right); Taiga/Shutterstock.com, p. 7; Hans Heinz/Shutterstock.com, pp. 9, 23 (bottom right); Standret/Shutterstock.com, p. 10; Coatesy/Shutterstock.com, pp. 12–13, 23 (bottom left); Artic_photo/Shutterstock.com, p. 14; Nik Merkulov/Shutterstock.com, pp. 17, 23 (top right); LeManna/Shutterstock.com, pp. 18–19; Marp51/Shutterstock.com, p. 21; Laura Westlund/Independent Picture Service, p. 22.

Cover: FotoHelin/Shutterstock.com.